AF268617

Macbeth - Pocket Study Guide

Written and illustrated by Tenille Dowe

First Printing, 2026

Published by Creative Heart Connection

www.creativeheartconnection.com

ISBN 978-1-7641624-6-3

Macbeth

Pocket Study Guide

By Tenille Dowe

Macbeth

Macbeth's Tragic Journey

Act 1 – Ambition Awakens
Macbeth hears the witches' prophecies and begins to imagine himself as king.

Act 2 – The Murder of Duncan
Pushed by Lady Macbeth, he kills King Duncan and immediately becomes overwhelmed by guilt and fear.

Act 3 – Descent into Tyranny
Now king, Macbeth orders Banquo's murder and becomes increasingly paranoid as he loses his moral control.

Act 4 – False Confidence
The witches' new prophecies give Macbeth a dangerous sense of invincibility, leading him to commit even greater violence.

Act 5 – Downfall and Death
Macbeth faces rebellion, loses everything, and is ultimately killed by Macduff, bringing his tragic journey to an end.

Lady Macbeth

Lady Macbeth

Act 1 – Ambitious Instigator
Lady Macbeth receives Macbeth's letter and immediately commits herself to helping him become king, calling on dark forces to "unsex" her and strengthen her resolve.

Act 2 – Driving the Murder
She takes control of the plan to kill Duncan, steadying Macbeth's nerves, placing the daggers, and ensuring the murder is covered up.

Act 3 – Cracks Beneath the Surface
Although she attempts to maintain control, especially during the banquet, Lady Macbeth begins to struggle as Macbeth becomes more secretive and violent.

Act 4 – Fading Influence
Lady Macbeth disappears from the centre of events as Macbeth's tyranny grows, and her earlier strength gives way to emotional and psychological strain.

Act 5 – Consumed by Guilt
Her guilt erupts into sleepwalking, obsessive hand-washing, and complete psychological collapse, leading to her off-stage death and marking the tragic cost of her ambition.

MacDuff

MacDuff

Act 1 – A Quiet but Loyal Thane
Macduff is introduced as a respected Scottish noble who is loyal to King Duncan and wary of unusual events surrounding Macbeth.

Act 2 – First to Suspect Foul Play
After Duncan's murder, Macduff immediately doubts Macbeth's story and refuses to attend his coronation, showing early suspicion and moral integrity.

Act 3 – Standing Apart from Macbeth's Rule
As Macbeth becomes increasingly tyrannical, Macduff distances himself and secretly travels to England to seek help from Malcolm.

Act 4 – Grief Turned to Resolve
Macduff learns that Macbeth has murdered his entire family, and his overwhelming grief transforms into a determined commitment to overthrow Macbeth.

Act 5 – The Hero Who Ends the Tyranny
Macduff kills Macbeth in the final battle, fulfilling the prophecy and restoring rightful leadership to Scotland.

Banquo

Banquo

Act 1 – The Cautious Observer
Banquo hears the witches' prophecies alongside Macbeth but responds with scepticism, warning that evil forces often tell partial truths to lead people to harm.

Act 2 – Loyal to Duncan, Steady in Honour
He remains loyal to King Duncan and quietly concerned about Macbeth's reaction to the prophecies, choosing integrity over ambition.

Act 3 – A Threat to Macbeth's Power
Because Macbeth fears the prophecy about Banquo's descendants becoming kings, Banquo becomes a target and is murdered on Macbeth's orders.

Act 4 – A Symbol of Macbeth's Guilt
Banquo's ghost appears at the banquet, exposing Macbeth's overwhelming guilt and mental decline in front of the court.

Act 5 – Legacy Beyond Death
Although Banquo is gone, his legacy continues through Fleance, whose escape keeps alive the prophecy that his line will one day rule Scotland.

Fleance

Fleance

Act 1 – Silent Witness to Prophecy
Fleance appears with Banquo when the witches' prophecies spark Macbeth's ambition, becoming part of the future they foretell.

Act 2 – A Loyal Son
He stays close to Banquo and follows his guidance, unaware of the growing danger surrounding Macbeth's rise to power.

Act 3 – Target of Macbeth's Fear
Because the witches predicted that Banquo's descendants would be kings, Fleance becomes a threat to Macbeth and is targeted in the assassination plot.

Act 4 – The Escape That Changes Everything
Fleance escapes the murderers, ensuring Macbeth cannot erase the prophecy and deepening Macbeth's paranoia and insecurity.

Act 5 – A Future Unwritten
Though absent from the action, Fleance's survival keeps alive the possibility that Banquo's line will one day rule Scotland, shaping the play's sense of destiny beyond its ending.

The
Witches

The Witches

Act 1 – The Prophecy Begins
The witches reveal three prophecies that spark Macbeth's ambition and set the tragic events in motion.

Act 2 – The Unseen Manipulators
Although they do not appear, their earlier words continue to influence Macbeth's choices and fuel his growing guilt.

Act 3 – Masters of Fate and Chaos
Hecate scolds the witches and directs them to mislead Macbeth further, strengthening their role in manipulating his downfall.

Act 4 – Deceptive Visions
They summon spirits that deliver twisted prophecies, giving Macbeth false confidence and pushing him toward even greater violence.

Act 5 – Their Influence Unravels
The witches' predictions come true in unexpected ways, proving they have shaped Macbeth's fate but ultimately cannot save him from destruction.

Act 1, Scene 1

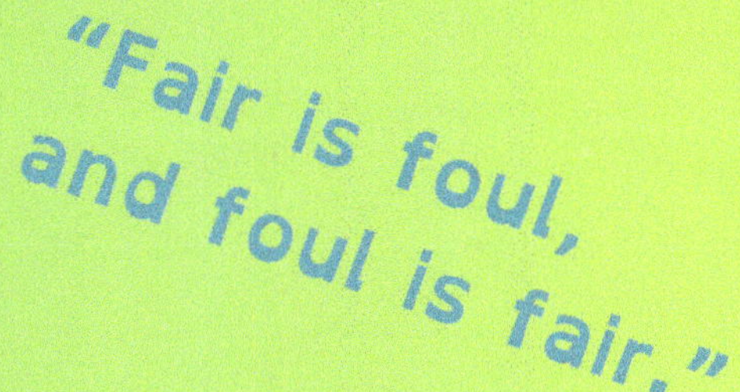

Technique
Antimetabole: A phrase repeated in reverse order for emphasis
Equivocation: Deliberately using unclear or misleading language to hide the truth.

Analysis: Establishes moral inversion and deception as central motifs. Appearance vs reality becomes the play's governing tension.

Context: Jacobean belief in witchcraft; fear of disorder under James I of England.

Link to Tragic Form: Foreshadows a world out of balance, a hallmark of Shakespearean tragedy.

Act 1, Scene 2

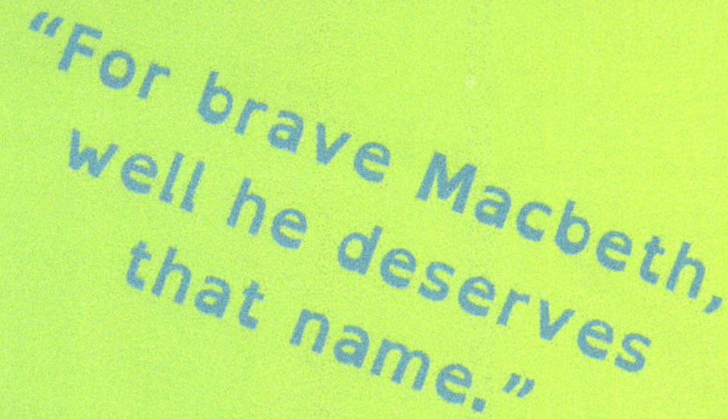

Technique
Epithet: A descriptive phrase that highlights a key quality of a person.
Dramatic irony: When the audience knows something important that the characters do not.

Analysis: Establishes Macbeth as a noble, loyal warrior

Context: Jacobean values of honour, loyalty to the king, and martial bravery under James I of England.

Link to Tragic Form: Establishes the tragic hero at a height of honour before his hamartia (ambition) leads to peripeteia and eventual downfall, reinforcing the classical tragic arc from greatness to ruin.

"All hail, Macbeth! Hail to thee,
Thane of Glamis!
All hail, Macbeth! Hail to thee,
Thane of Cawdor!
All hail, Macbeth,
that shalt be king hereafter!"
Act 1, Scene 3

> "All hail, Macbeth! Hail to thee,
> Thane of Glamis!
> All hail, Macbeth! Hail to thee,
> Thane of Cawdor!
> All hail, Macbeth,
> that shalt be king hereafter!"

Technique

Repetition: Reusing a word or phrase to emphasise an idea or feeling.

Equivocation: Deliberately using unclear or misleading language to hide the truth.

Analysis: The triple salutation elevates Macbeth and ignites his ambition. The rhythmic repetition creates a hypnotic, almost ritualistic tone, emphasising supernatural influence.

Context: Jacobean fear of witchcraft, particularly under James I of England, who had a strong interest in demonology.

Link to Tragic Form: This is the inciting moment of the tragedy, fate tempts the tragic hero, activating his hamartia (ambition) and setting the irreversible chain of events in motion.

"So foul and fair a day I have not seen."
Act 1, Scene 3

Technique
Paradox: A statement that seems impossible or contradictory but reveals a deeper truth.

Analysis: Echoes the witches, aligning Macbeth with chaos before he realises it. This verbal mirroring symbolically links him to the supernatural before he even meets them.

Context: Suggests susceptibility to supernatural influence.

Link to Tragic Form: Signals the tragic hero's entanglement with fate.

"Stars, hide your fires; Let not light see my black and deep desires."
(Aside)
Act 1, Scene 4

Technique

Imagery: Descriptive language that creates a strong picture or sensory experience in the reader's mind.

Metaphor: A comparison saying one thing is another to create deeper meaning.

Analysis: Reveals ambition and moral awareness. He knows his desire is "black."

Context: Divine Right of Kings, regicide is a sin against God.

Link to Tragic Form: Introduction of hamartia (fatal flaw - ambition).

"Come, you spirits
That tend on mortal
thoughts, unsex me here,
And fill me from the crown
to the toe top-full Of
direst cruelty!"
Act 1, Scene 5

Technique

Metaphor: A comparison saying one thing is another to create deeper meaning.

Imagery: Descriptive language that creates a strong picture or sensory experience in the reader's mind.

Analysis: Lady Macbeth calls on supernatural forces to strip her of femininity, so she can commit ruthless acts. The language emphasises her ambition and rejection of societal gender norms, highlighting her influence over Macbeth.

Context: Upon reading Macbeth's letter about the witches' prophecy; reflects Jacobean anxieties about female power and ambition.

Link to Tragic Form: Sets the stage for Macbeth's downfall by introducing external manipulation. Lady Macbeth becomes a catalyst for Macbeth's hamartia.

"I have no spur
To prick the sides of my
intent, but only
vaulting ambition."
ambition
Act 1, Scene 7

Technique
Extended metaphor: A comparison that continues over several lines or throughout part of a text.
Imagery: Descriptive language that creates a strong picture or sensory experience in the reader's mind.

Analysis: Macbeth recognises that ambition alone drives him. The image of over-leaping suggests inevitable self-destruction.

Context: Soliloquy debating whether to kill Duncan.

Link to Tragic Form: Self-awareness of fatal flaw, classic tragic hero moment.

Act 1, Scene 7

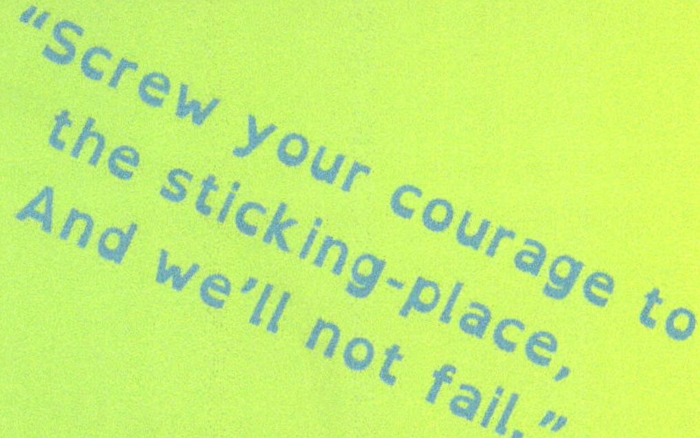

Technique
Metaphor: A comparison saying one thing is another to create deeper meaning.

Analysis: Lady Macbeth urges Macbeth to be resolute in killing King Duncan. Her words reinforce the commitment to ruthless ambition and demonstrate her psychological control.

Context: She manipulates his insecurity, fear and ambition.

Link to Tragic Form: Shows the combination of internal flaw (ambition) and external pressure (Lady Macbeth) driving the hero toward irreversible tragic consequences.

"Is this a dagger which I see before me......?"
Act 2, Scene 1

Technique
Soliloquy: A speech where a character speaks their thoughts aloud while alone on stage.
Hallucination: A false sensory experience where someone sees or hears something that isn't really there.
Symbolism: When an object, image, or action represents a deeper meaning or idea.

Analysis: Blurs reality and imagination; guilt manifests visually.

Context: Supernatural ambiguity, psychological vs demonic influence.

Link to Tragic Form: Internal conflict before the irreversible act.

"Will all great Neptune's ocean wash this blood clean from my hand?"
Act 2, Scene, 2

Technique
Hyperbole: Deliberate exaggeration used for emphasis or effect.

Classical allusion: A reference to myths, history, or literature.

Analysis: Blood symbolises guilt; crime is spiritually permanent.

Context: Renaissance belief in divine justice. God is the ultimate judge.

Link to Tragic Form: Recognition of moral consequence begins.

"Me thought I heard a voice cry 'Sleep no more! Macbeth does murder sleep.'"
Act 2, Scene 2

> *"Me thought I heard a voice cry*
> *'Sleep no more!*
> *Macbeth does murder sleep.'"*

Technique
Personification: Giving human qualities to non-human things.
Motif (sleep): A recurring image, idea, or pattern that helps develop themes in a text.
Auditory hallucination: Hearing sounds or voices that are not actually present.

Analysis: Sleep symbolises innocence and peace. By murdering Duncan, Macbeth destroys his own ability to rest, foreshadowing guilt and paranoia.

Context: Immediately after the murder.
Link to Tragic Form: Shows psychological consequences of hamartia, guilt begins to consume him.

"A little water clears us of this deed."

Act 2, Scene 2

Technique
Dramatic irony: When the audience knows something important that the characters do not.
Symbolism: (water vs blood) When an object, image, or action represents a deeper meaning or idea.

Analysis: Lady Macbeth minimises the crime, believing it can be easily erased. Ironically, she will later be unable to wash away imagined blood ("Out, damned spot!").

Context: She is attempting to calm Macbeth after Duncan's murder.

Link to Tragic Form: Highlights reversal, her early confidence contrasts with later madness, reinforcing the tragic trajectory.

"I go, and it is done; the bell invites me."
Act 2, Scene 1

Technique
Personification: Giving human qualities to non-human things.
Symbolism: When an object, image, or action represents a deeper meaning or idea.

Analysis: The bell becomes a summons to murder and damnation. This line marks the final step from thought to action.

Context: Immediately before killing King Duncan.

Link to Tragic Form: Point of no return, the irreversible act that propels the tragic arc.

"To be thus is nothing; But to be safely thus."
Act 3, Scene 1

Technique
Paradox: A statement that seems impossible or contradictory but reveals a deeper truth.
Repetition: Reusing a word or phrase to emphasise an idea or feeling.

Analysis: Being king means nothing without security. This marks a second turning point, Macbeth now initiates violence independently, planning Banquo's murder.

Context: Fear of Banquo and the prophecy about Fleance becoming king.

Link to Tragic Form: Shift from tragic hero to tyrant, ambition evolves into paranoia and moral decay.

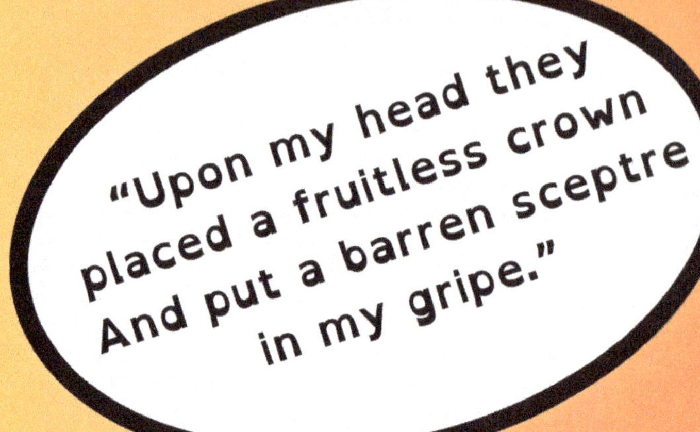

"Upon my head they
placed a fruitless crown
And put a barren sceptre
in my gripe."

Act 3, Scene 1

Technique

Metaphor: A comparison saying one thing is another to create deeper meaning.

Imagery: Descriptive language that creates a strong picture or sensory experience in the reader's mind.

Symbolism: When an object, image, or action represents a deeper meaning or idea.

Analysis: Macbeth acknowledges that his kingship is meaningless if it produces no heirs. His obsession with legacy intensifies his ambition and justifies more violence.

Context: Reflecting on the prophecy and the threat Banquo's descendants pose.

Link to Tragic Form: Hamlet-like obsession with securing the future, hamartia (uncontrolled ambition) now dictates all actions.

"We hear our bloody cousins
are bestowed,
In England and in Ireland, not
confessing,
Their cruel parricide."
Act 3, Scene 1

Technique

Euphemism: A polite or mild phrase used to replace something harsh or unpleasant.

Dramatic irony: When the audience knows something important that the characters do not.

Analysis: Macbeth rationalises violence as necessary to secure his power. His ambition now justifies preemptive murder (Banquo and Fleance), showing moral decline from hesitant murderer to calculating tyrant.

Context: He refers to Malcolm and Donalbain after King Duncan's death, fearing their survival threatens his crown.

Link to Tragic Form: Demonstrates escalation of hamartia, ambition drives increasingly destructive and irreversible actions.

"O, full of
scorpions is my
mind, dear wife!"
Act 3, Scene 2

Technique

Metaphor: A comparison saying one thing is another to create deeper meaning.

Symbolism: When an object, image, or action represents a deeper meaning or idea.

Analysis: Macbeth compares his thoughts to scorpions, suggesting his mind is poisoned with fear, paranoia and violence. Unlike earlier hesitation, he now independently plots Banquo's murder, showing ambition transforming into tyrannical power. The imagery conveys psychological torment and loss of inner peace.

Context: He has secured the crown but feels no safety, because he believes the prophecy.

Link to Tragic Form: Progression from hamartia (ambition) to moral corruption and psychological disintegration.

Act 3, Scene 3

Technique
Repetition: Reusing a word or phrase to emphasise an idea or feeling.

Analysis: Spoken by Banquo during the ambush, this quote highlights the danger Macbeth has created through his ambition. Macbeth orders his murder, Fleance's escape intensifies Macbeth's paranoia, driving him toward further ruthless acts.

Context: Macbeth has hired murderers to kill Banquo and Fleance to prevent the prophecy about Banquo's heir becoming King.

Link to Tragic Form: Shows consequences of the hero's hamartia spreading beyond himself. Ambition causes escalating violence, a key element of a tragedy.

"Thou canst not say I did it!"
Act 3, Scene 4

Technique
Hallucination: Hearing or seeing something that isn't really there.
Supernatural imagery: Descriptions involving ghosts, witches, magic, or forces beyond the natural world.
Emotive outburst: A sudden expression of strong emotion, usually uncontrolled.

Analysis: Macbeth's denial to the ghost shows his collapsing sanity and desperate attempt to avoid responsibility.

Context: Macbeth has ordered Banquo's murder, and the banquet exposes the psychological consequences of his actions.

Link to Tragic Form: The moment demonstrates Macbeth's fatal flaw driving him toward inevitable downfall, a key element of tragedy.

"The table's full."
Act 3, Scene 4

Technique
Hallucination: Hearing or seeing something that isn't really there.
Dramatic Irony: When the audience knows something important that the characters do not.

Analysis: He thinks Banquo's ghost is sitting in his place, even though no one else sees it.
The guests do not know why Macbeth is acting strangely, but the audience knows he is guilty of killing Banquo.

Context: Banquo has been killed (Macbeth ordered this to happen).

Link to Tragic Form: This moment shows Macbeth losing control in public, marking the beginning of his tragic downfall.

'It will have blood, they say; blood will have blood.'
Act 3, Scene 4

> *"It will have blood, they say; blood will have blood."*

Technique
Foreshadowing: A hint or clue about events that will happen later in the story.
Repetition: Reusing a word or phrase to emphasise an idea or feeling.

Analysis: Macbeth realises that his murders will bring consequences and that he cannot escape the cycle of bloodshed.

Context: He says this after seeing Banquo's ghost, which makes him fear that his crimes are starting to catch up with him.

Link to Tragic Form: This moment shows Macbeth understanding his fatal mistake too late, pushing him further toward his tragic downfall.

"Macbeth! Macbeth! Macbeth! beware Macduff; Beware the thane of Fife."
1
Act 4, Scene 1

"Macbeth! Macbeth! Macbeth! beware Macduff; Beware the thane of Fife."

Technique
Repetition: Reusing a word or phrase to emphasise an idea or feeling.
Prophecy: A prediction about the future, often connected to fate or the supernatural.

Analysis: The warning intensifies Macbeth's paranoia. He becomes obsessed with eliminating threats, showing ambition turning into tyrannical insecurity.

Context: The witches show apparitions to manipulate Macbeth.

Link to Tragic Form: The prophecy motivates further moral decay, escalating toward catastrophe.

"None of woman born shall harm Macbeth."
2
Act 4, Scene 1

Technique
Equivocation: Deliberately using unclear or misleading language to hide the truth.
Dramatic irony: When the audience knows something important that the characters do not.

Analysis: False security through ambiguous prophecy.

Context: Fear of deceptive language (linked to post-Gunpowder Plot anxieties).

Link to Tragic Form: Hubris driven by misinterpretation of fate.

"By the pricking of my thumbs, something wicked this way comes."
Act 4, Scene 1

"By the pricking of my thumbs, something wicked this way comes."

Technique
Foreshadowing: A hint or clue about events that will happen later in the story.
Dramatic irony: The audience knows something important that the characters do not.
Personification: Giving human qualities to non-human things.

Analysis: The witches sense Macbeth's moral corruption, he has become "wicked" in their eyes. This shows his transformation from hesitant murderer to ruthless tyrant.

Context: Macbeth approaches the witches to learn more about his fate.

Link to Tragic Form: Highlights the hero's full descent into moral evil, his ambition now overrides conscience.

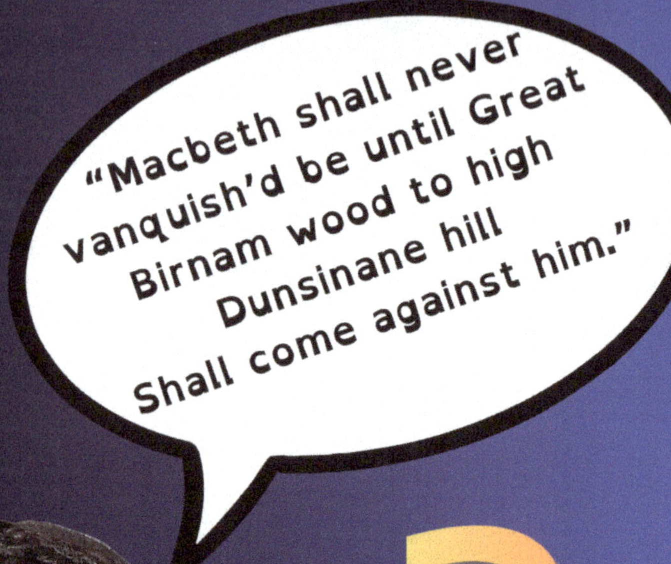

"Macbeth shall never
vanquish'd be until Great
Birnam wood to high
Dunsinane hill
Shall come against him."
3
Act 4, Scene 1

"Macbeth shall never vanquish'd be until Great Birnam wood to high Dunsinane hill Shall come against him."

Technique
Dramatic irony: The audience knows something important that the characters do not.
Personification: Giving human qualities to non-human things.
Metaphor: A comparison saying one thing is another to create deeper meaning.

Analysis: Another ambiguous prophecy that inflates Macbeth's confidence. His ambition blinds him to reality, leading to overreach.

Context: The witches are manipulating Macbeth with riddling predictions.

Link to Tragic Form: Reinforces tragic irony, the hero's misinterpretation of fate propels him toward catastrophe.

"Your castle is surprised; your wife and babes Savagely slaughter'd." (Ross)
Act 4, Scene 3

Technique

Emotive language: Words chosen to make the reader feel a strong emotion.

Violent imagery: Descriptions that show harm, bloodshed, or physical aggression.

Analysis: This language shows Macbeth's complete moral collapse and creates strong sympathy for Macduff and highlights the brutality of the murder of Macduff's innocent "wife and babes."

Tragic Form & Context

The killing violates Jacobean beliefs about natural and social order, reinforcing Macbeth's role as a tyrant whose downfall is inevitable in the tragic structure.

"Out, damned spot! Out, I say!"
Act 5, Scene 1

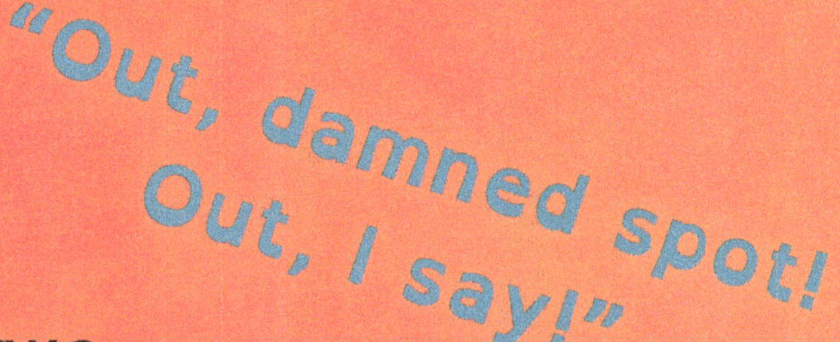

Technique
Symbolism: When an object, image, or action represents a deeper meaning or idea.
Fragmented prose: Broken, incomplete, or disjointed sentences that reflect confusion or distress.

Analysis: Guilt overwhelms her; reversal of earlier strength.

Context: Madness as punishment; breakdown of unnatural ambition.

Link to Tragic Form: Peripeteia and psychological collapse.

"Tomorrow, and tomorrow, and tomorrow..."
Act 5, Scene 5

Technique

Repetition: Reusing a word or phrase to emphasise an idea or feeling.

Imagery: Descriptive language that creates a strong picture or sensory experience in the reader's mind.

Metaphor: A comparison saying one thing is another to create deeper meaning.

Analysis: Life reduced to meaninglessness; existential despair.

Context: After Lady Macbeth's death; isolation of the tyrant.

Link to Tragic Form: Anagnorisis recognition of the emptiness of his ambition.

"Macduff was from his mother's womb untimely ripp'd."
Act 5, Scene 8

Technique
Dramatic irony: The audience knows something important that the characters do not.
Equivocation: Deliberately using unclear or misleading language to hide the truth.
Revelation: A sudden realisation or discovery of an important truth.

Analysis: This line reveals that Macduff was born by Caesarean section, meaning he was not technically "of woman born." The witches' prophecy is fulfilled in an unexpected way. Macbeth's false sense of security collapses instantly.

Context: The prophecy from the Witches in Act 4 is exposed as deceptive.

Link to Tragic Form: This is the moment of anagnorisis (recognition), Macbeth realises he has been misled and that his fate is sealed.

"I'll fight till from my bones my flesh be hack'd."
Act 5, Scene 3

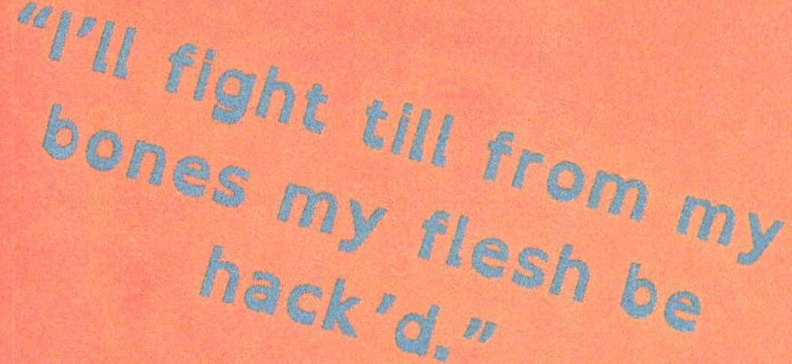

Technique
Violent imagery: Descriptions that show harm, bloodshed, or physical aggression.
Hyperbole: Deliberate exaggeration used for emphasis or effect.

Analysis: Macbeth clings to power through brute force. Even as Scotland turns against him, he refuses surrender. His ambition has transformed into blind defiance. He would rather be destroyed than yield the throne.

Context: He is isolated, abandoned by many thanes, and increasingly tyrannical.

Link to Tragic Form: Shows hubris and stubborn refusal to recognise his inevitable downfall.

"Lay on, Macduff."
Act 5, Scene 8

"Lay on, Macduff."

Technique
Imperative: A command or instruction telling someone to do something.
Tragic defiance: A hero's refusal to give up, even when facing certain doom.

Analysis: Returns to warrior identity; faces consequences.

Context: Restoration of natural order through Macduff.

Link to Tragic Form: Catastrophe, death of the tragic hero and moral restoration.

"Hail, King! for so thou art. Behold, where stands The usurper's cursed head."
Act 5, Scene 8

Technique
Symbolism: When an object, image, or action represents a deeper meaning or idea.

Analysis: Macduff shows that justice has been served by killing Macbeth and proving the tyrant is gone.

Context: Macduff returns after killing Macbeth and presents his head to Malcolm.

Link to Tragic Form: Macbeth's death completes his tragic downfall, showing how his ambition ultimately destroys him and restores order.

Vocabulary List with Definitions

Metaphor – A comparison saying one thing is another to create deeper meaning.

Imagery – Descriptive language that creates a strong picture or sensory experience in the reader's mind.

Antimetabole – A phrase repeated in reverse order for emphasis (e.g., "Fair is foul, and foul is fair").

Equivocation – Deliberately using unclear or misleading language to hide the truth.

Epithet – A descriptive label or phrase that highlights a key quality of a person or thing.

Heroic imagery – Language that portrays a character as noble, brave, or larger-than-life.

Dramatic irony – When the audience knows something important that the characters do not.

Repetition – Reusing a word or phrase to emphasise an idea or feeling.

Paradox – A statement that seems impossible or contradictory but reveals a deeper truth.

Extended metaphor – A comparison that continues over several lines or throughout part of a text.

Hallucination – A false sensory experience where someone sees or hears something that isn't really there.

Soliloquy – A speech where a character speaks their thoughts aloud while alone on stage.

Symbolism – When an object, image, or action represents a deeper meaning or idea.

Hyperbole – Deliberate exaggeration used for emphasis or effect.

Classical allusion – A reference to myths, history, or literature.

Motif – A recurring image, idea, or pattern that helps develop themes in a text.

Personification – Giving human qualities to non-human things.

Auditory hallucination – Hearing sounds or voices that are not actually present.

Euphemism – A polite or mild phrase used to replace something harsh or unpleasant.

Emotive outburst – A sudden expression of strong emotion, usually uncontrolled.

Prophecy – A prediction about the future, often connected to fate or the supernatural.

Foreshadowing – A hint or clue about events that will happen later in the story.

Emotive language – Words chosen to make the reader feel a strong emotion.

Violent imagery – Descriptions that show harm, bloodshed, or physical aggression.

Fragmented prose – Broken, incomplete, or disjointed sentences that reflect confusion or distress.

Revelation – A sudden realisation or discovery of an important truth.

Imperative – A command or instruction telling someone to do something.

Tragic defiance – A hero's refusal to give up, even when facing certain doom.

Rhetorical question – A question asked for effect, not because an answer is expected.

Peripeteia – The turning point where the character's fortune reverses from good to bad.

Hamartia – A character's fatal mistake or error in judgment that leads to their downfall.

Hubris – Excessive pride or arrogance that blinds a character to danger.

The Great Chain of Being – The belief that everything in the universe has a fixed, God-given place in a natural hierarchy.

Regicide – The act of killing a king.

Usurpation – Taking power or a position that does not rightfully belong to you.

Divine Right of Kings – The belief that a king's power comes directly from God and cannot be questioned.

Tragic flaw – A weakness in a character's personality that contributes to their downfall.

Supernatural imagery – Descriptions involving ghosts, witches, magic, or forces beyond the natural world.

Notes & Quotes

www.ingramcontent.com/pod-product-compliance
Lightning Source LLC
Chambersburg PA
CBHW050037040726
47599CB00015B/1726